CARRYIN

COPY RIG

JENNIFER LORRAINE ALEXANDER

FIRST PRINTING, 2020

ISBN: 9798657226515

Imprint: Independently published

Carrying a Dead Man's Weight

Goal for this book:

A sinner to accept Jesus Christ as their personal LORD and Saviour

Contents

Contents

Prayer for Protection

O Lord, Father, in the name of Jesus
God, I pray for the audience and me
Forgive those who have despised and wronged us
And forgive us when we sin against thee
Jesus, I pray this prayer of protection
That we may remain shielded in Your arm
Help lead the people in Your direction
I plead the blood of Jesus against harm
O LORD, we need you like never before
To deliver us from the wicked one
Humbly postured, our face to the floor
Present Help, the only Begotten Son
Make our enemies to be like the wind
We pray in the name of Jesus, Amen.

Angels Battling

They gather together against the saints

Viewed a history search and back ground check

Applying pressure to make the saints wreck

Given limited time to watch them tank

Wanted to wash away their smile they paint

Followers of Christ, love without regret

Even when their hated up to their necks

Enemies of Christ, somehow always faint

Jesus lovers use spiritual weapons

Prayers are bullets, the Word of God, a sword

Rats, serpents will forever be threatened

Incorruptible crown is the reward

Michael is warring for saints in heaven

Fact of the matter, Jesus is LORD.

Christ is calling

God heard what you said while you were praying,
"I repent of my sins" but you straying.
From solid truth which is the word of God,
Don't pay tithes criminal at heart, you rob.
Repentance means nothing if you don't change,
Plead the blood of Jesus, this ain't a game.
Cancel assignments that you can't handle,
Bind the enemy hands up, dismantled.
You know how to pray yet Satan's still there,
Things don't go your way; you say life ain't fair.
Remember scriptures, your confidence boost,
But you still not saved running round here loose.
One thing I can attest while you're in wait,
Christ wants to save you before it's too late.

Regimented

We summoned you in under false pretense,
Wanted to know your motive and intent.
Test after test some you past, others failed,
The loyalty you've shown has taught us well.
Changed your perspective about life itself,
Grew up before our eyes, did it yourself.
Sacrifices made receiving your kind,
Death threats if you leave, we put in your mind.
Tamed that slick talking and gave you tickets,
Tried to stunt on us but you heard crickets.
A hit list was made guess who was on top,
Kill, steal and destroy, we schemed and made plots.
Now that you're one of us, what can we say?
Another warrior ready to spray.

He Spoke

He spoke life over dead situations

He spoke decrees over declarations

He spoke to the water as the boat rocked

He spoke peace across the land to His flock

He spoke words of victory during trials

He spoke nothing as He stumbled those miles

He spoke to me personally through praise

He spoke about comforting all my days

He spoke patience, accountability

He spoke knowledge with more humility

He spoke while two loaves, five fish were given

He spoke in love then sins were forgiven

He spoke in the present about the past

He spoke the bible which will never pass

Murder In The House

Stanzas written are as bullets loaded

Each word cocked back killing readers' noted

My sonnets can spray you down, Ms AK

Ten syllables a line, spit in your face

Dressed in all black, there's no rhythm to this

Murder in the house, ain't no stopping it

Background scenery, midnight twelve A.M

Mourning's can also be in the P.M

Never been a killer except with words

Taste my thoughts; you'll vomit from what you heard

A pen with ink is my only weapon

Murder in the house, making bread leaven

I had fun with this just to prove a point

Weed smokers could've got high to this joint

What's in the Kitchen?

What’s in the kitchen? Who’s cooking dinner?

Notes of order, the chief and head waiter.

Empty plastic cups ready to be filled.

A deep freezer that’s made from stainless steel.

Two microwaves, one of which is broken.

An oven stove that’s no longer smokin’

What’s in the kitchen, you ask once again?

Recycled Keurig pot brewing caffeine.

Stained dirty dishes are in the kitchen.

To do list: clogged pipes need a fixin’.

Refrigerator, cupboard and freezer.

Geezer, sneaker, reefer, rhymes with ether.

Who’s in the kitchen? Few hungry people.

Demolishing food that’s an acquittal.

Call It Out

When I first got it, I thought "this is fresh"

Started to hear too much, it became stress

I heard other people's conversation

Beginnings' end, Book of Lamentation

Who wants a gift like this, hearing voices

Yall think I'm crazy; yeah that's why I rejoice

Walk into a room thoughts bouncing off walls

Belittle me in your mind, think I'm small

You know how hard it is writing this poem

I AM NOT A PSYCHIC, I AM NOT THEM

From me to yall, it's a form of witchcraft

I joke about it so people just laugh

I'm exposing it so I can escape

Tired of *Carrying a Dead Man's Weight*

My Messy Self

I’m confused and difficult to deal with,

Sit on the front row of the church, pulpit.

Destructive to peers also family,

I get a kick out of being messy.

My ways are complex; they’ll leave you tangled,

I’m all over the nation, star bangles.

Mrs. Petty doesn’t compare to my name,

The one starting rumors, I’ll never change.

Opposite of ordered and uncluttered,

Just like canned collard greens, I’m mustard.

Taste grimy at times when I’m in your mouth,

Get upset quick when sent another route.

Even the angels cried when Jesus wept,

On each pew in church with my messy self.

I AM ADULTERY

Different assignments over my life

Calling him bro, while flirting with his wife

Checking the background is a major start

What's love when it doesn't come from the heart?

I'm assigned to come break up which remains

He's busy working while she's playing games

Truth be told I don't want to destroy homes

She's tired of you always being gone

Not realizing her pain, hurts me as well

Purple Heart for war, right now it looks pale

Wasn't assigned to make yall look as fools

He made it easy for me being cruel

Pretentious vows before monogamy

Assignment fulfilled: I AM ADULTERY

Love Thy Neighbors

Friday nights the worse, yall be arguing
In my earlobe, I can hear yall fussing
Every other day it's something new
Say yall in love but why he hit on you
Understand life is stress, we all get that
There's no excuse for your eye being black
He's head of house yet to him, you ain't worth
Two pots to piss in; He treats you like dirt.
Call cops, press charges, next day charges dropped
It's habit for yall, that's why he won't stop
Beating on you. It irks my nerves to hear
When he raises his voice then cracks a beer
I'm hoping he get his act together
Girl, don't you tolerate this forever

Life Without Dad

I was born to live a life without dad
Grew up with father figures is what I had
Mom was there for me each step of the way
I celebrated mom on Father's day
Asked myself, "why I don't have a father?"
No grandparents, no pops, I was bothered
Debutante ball, a cousin danced with me
He was the substitute; I was angry
All that time I thought dad wasn't a live
Pops don't wana see me, I feel deprived
We talk on the phone and that's about it
We trying to meet? I'm about to quit
He won't even send pictures of himself
A life without dad, I have no regrets

5one5

When I saw you I knew you were the one

Real laid back, quiet and love to have fun

A lot in common, I wasn't surprised

Leader on board, it would be me you drive

From another city, don't look your age

Growing out the TWA stage

Exchanged words cause I got in my feelings

No emergency stops, guess who trippin'

Now we barely speak so I'll take the blame

I can see you shine past the storm and rain

Even though there was no real connection

Truthfully I'm tired of rejection

Back of my mind want to say, "forget you"

Yep, you guessed it, this poem is about you

I’m Assigned to You

Behind enemies' line, you were picked out

Summoned you from what you said out your mouth

In your presence I'll present quick gestures

I heard the words you spoke, yes it festered

Doing all I could to make things look cool

During that time, it was your soul I ruled

Captain of the van so no one checked me

And your life was spared this time luckily

Remember the dream, your cards were stolen?

You caught me but my hands smooth as lotion

Took one step further going to your house

Brought two other people, mission aroused

For extra points I've been working this poem

You wrote about me, middle of a storm

Hello, Schizo

Counting my fingers like one, two, three, four

Anxious when paper is on carpet floors

Talk in circles so things make common sense

Tired of seeing nine one one sequence

Scream aloud when given many commands

Make people look when I sound like a man

Twirling my hair while staring into space

Hoping not to lose my mind in that place

Right heel moving accelerated tap

Another episode second relapse

Touching my nose like a baby button

Voices in my head talking back fussin'

This poem could be a figment of my mind

Until I look at a clock to tell time

Mummy's Daughter

Mummy’s daughter isn’t breathing, she’s dead

Carrying a Dead Man’s Weight! Published, read.

Several months of housing withered child

Those were months of joy the mother could smile

Innocent child born in a cruel world

Fetal death or still born, that’s what occurred

Mummy was unemotional to death

The drugs she took destroyed her unborn' health

Treat a dead body as desecrated corps

Patches of emotions preserved balm warts

The look in mummy’s eyes no one could see

Unattended child is dead weight to she

Mummy’s daughter was big as a boiled egg

Mummy’s daughter isn’t breathing, she’s dead

C-U-2

Crisis unit mode, they say I'm crazy

If a stare could kill, my eyes are lazy

Hit man retired, this is not the time

To assonate character, old wine

Hennessey cognac, dark liquor no chase

I don't know dude name, but I know his face

The guy with tattoos, 'Hello Jennifer'

Purple shirt, brown pants, there wasn't murder

Mickey Mouse hairstyle, I remember you

Sent friend request, guess it didn't go through

Why Mister Dread head, my cup is half full

Filling me up with psych meds, I refuel

Sitting in bed; sad, the last man standing

Second visit here with second chances

Letter of Appreciation (Never Sent)

Thank you for showing in attendance

We appreciate the money you spent

Thank you for every message you gave

A form of humbleness, the beaten slave

Thank you for participating when used

Hurt in different ways, the child abused

As your leaders, we thought you'll turn out fine

In the midnight hour the moon still shines

Keeping your mouth shut, we thank you the most

Our special child whom we wouldn't let boast

We appreciate you promoting us

Especially the bench plus other stuff

Even though these words never came to you

For all of your hard work, we say thank you

A Whore's Prayer

Lord, this time with you I cannot pretend,

What's in my mouth? Unforgivable sin.

I've created wars within my own self,

I cannot remember the day I left.

Your presence, to take on the walking dead,

Full of deceit carrying in my bed.

God, I'm not here to say that I'm sorry,

Time waits for no man, I sit and tarry.

Guilt and shame surface while writing this poem,

Tears being held back going through a storm.

I know it's you keeping me together,

Times I caused destruction, you're my shelter.

Father, should I ask forgiveness again?

Reprobate mind addicted to Jen's sin.

Stop Being So Touchy

"How you gon write about what you been through?

It's some deep stuff but foreal, I feel you.

I can't write a book describing my life,

You even wrote a poem bout a man's wife.

Poetry is your gift, readers unwrap.

I applaud your work, it really ain't crap.

Touching on subjects like this a bible,

Special leader without any title.

You wrote poems being saved while liking girls,

Abomination, you tell to the world."

From author to reader this means a lot.

See through my eyes, the areas I blot.

I've been silent so long because I'm hushed.

Whatever I can't say my words can touch.

Be Real With God

Forget nonsense I'm trying to be real

Show emotions that I don't even feel

Smile on my face when I'm telling the truth

All gas no breaks make it do what it do

Took me awhile to admit my own faults

Being real with God was a lesson taught

No time to argue but I will if need

Speak on what it is take this truth and feed

I'm not saying I won't tell lies again

What's lying to having sex? It's all sin.

I mean I asked Christ why I couldn't stop

He replied, "you love being on the top."

The devil heard us then he intervened

You have work to do without being seen

Take Up Your Bed

Pieces of my body graccfully broke

As the words in his mouth healed me and spoke,

“Wake up daughter your time has come full term

To be strengthened while standing your ground firm

I have given you milk for quite awhile

Take bread, eat meat, you’re no longer a child

Considering steps that’s been made thus far

Help me, help you remove visible scars

Pieces of your body given to men

They’ve touched you but you’re covered by my hand

A faithful servant over a few things

Not faithful enough to receive a ring.”

Thank you for leading me on a straight path

Your words healed me even in your wrath

Still Standing Still

Have you ever had paralyzing fear?

It makes you hold your breath and shed a tear

Literally can't move body frozen

Can't say nothing like vocals been stolen

Thoughts running through your head miles per hour

A bad taste on your tongue, bitter sour

Is it fear or a moment of silence?

Everyone else seems bright and vibrant

Snake's venom paralyzes its' victims

I won't be a product of the system

I hope when you read this, you move forward

"UNLATCH YOUR TEETH," that's the authors order

Years from now I'll be walking by faith till…

The Lord say "wait, be patient and be still"

Wrongfully Told

Officer, she followed me in the church

Staring at what I had on a blue skirt

I walked faster as she spoke to the guys

Officer, this all truth I tell no lies

When I put my purse down, she was right there

After looking down, she hand brushed her hair

Deacons were on standby in case she snapped

Blocked the exit, her foot began to tap

Jen opened her mouth this is what she said,

“I’m sent here to heal you, lemme give you head.”

Others heard it who were sitting near by

Officer she’s lost it or must be high

This what happened because I didn’t change

They consider me crazy and deranged

Stop Playing Victim

Victims are helpless and have been cheated,

Including suffered and feels defeated.

Also one who is wronged or unwitting.

Maybe a person who feels unfitting.

The victim in this case wasn't helpless,

Had plenty knowledge, feeding the flesh.

Evidence show signs of penetration,

Visible action participation.

Intuition was present at the scene,

Consciously awake during Halloween.

Tough decisions were made while sharing thoughts,

I tried to warn them without being caught.

Me? I am not the victim, I played too,

Every step of the way, I left clues.

Devils' Portals

Deceive them young because they like to touch

Virginities broken starting with lust

Forget about fasting days, suddenly

Use to be one plate, now two, gluttony

Slow to God but getting money with speed

Want to gain the world, fill their heart with greed

Talking to self so what's a psychopath?

Transfer energy so they deal with wrath

Nothing wrong with having good rivalries

Want what they have, its considered envy

Stroked egos are enlarged, where self can't hide

Seven colors, seven sins equal pride

They think they live forever, immortal

Small open gates are the devil's portals

Outsiders View

We sit in groups just to laugh at loners

The ones who isolate themselves, roamers

Our hellos turn into silent goodbyes

Walking in a daze with bloodshot wide eyes

Our clique never needed you anyway

Struggle written over the castaways

A simple smile can change everything soon

Go days without speaking, covered cocoon

Their highs are high and the lows are extreme

Face of contentment yet taken for mean

We chat about how loners look and sound

Even when they walk, face toward the ground

Because loners don't speak, we set them up

Wanting them to fail wishing for bad luck

Messed Up Reputation

Writing keeps me from calling that man's wife,

Exposing myself through this poem, I might.

Watching over her at church, no sexton,

Telling lies between thighs, fornication.

My wife thinks she's the only one I kiss,

Assigned to deceive woman, a snake's hiss.

Run game, play games pronounce words that allure,

A few lines a day then she let me score.

I've convinced myself writing keeps me home,

With my family so I do no wrong.

Then I think about that man's wife I've had,

Pamper the present to ignore the past.

We used each other, sex exploitation,

That sounds like a messed up reputation.

Slothfulness

Tell me why you stopped writing poetry?

Married to slothfulness, polygamy

It's a gift we have to share with others

Creativity is the supporter

The paper and pen are our major tools

Laziness and distractions make us fools

Knowing who we are as real messengers

Traveling the back road as a detour

In the wrong season to have writers' block

Be a vendor of words, time to restock

Plus, you've been in this place far too long

"Who wrote this poem?" aye, isn't that a song?

Don't be the person this poem is about

School of Writing is in, do not drop out

I Look Like

I look like the child who's been brought to shame

Hearing laughter in my mind left a stain

I look like a youth who's pushed to the edge

Pressured from peers creating a gapped wedge

I look like a young adult leaving home

Eager to explore the world on my own

I don't look like someone who's been dismayed

I AM VICTORY and defeat can't stay

I don't look like what my past brought me through

I AM LOVED my testimony is true

I don't look like someone's throw away doll

I AM WONDERFULLY MADE, fear must fall

I hope this doesn't seem like arrogance

God created all of us different

Bus Stop 5055

In blistering cold waiting on the bus,

Thinking bout family, I have no trust.

First week of January brand new me,

I don't want to be cold but its freezing.

Watching folks drive while I'm at the bus stop,

Writing another book, hope it don't flop.

Wearing hoop earrings and a grey hoodie,

This bi-polar weather makes me moody.

Been forty-five minutes, I'm still waiting,

What's taken so long can't feel my facin'.

Hands brick cold got me speaking through the phone,

Times like this put me in another zone.

Dedicated to this, chasing my dream,

My life's purpose ain't as far as it seems.

Out of Training

Work with different personalities

Answered food surveys satisfactory

Customer service over and beyond

Family business grandpa to grandson

Tardiness happens on rare occasions

Workaholics take mental vacations

Benefits aren't great but it's a job

Janitor on duty, can't have work slobs

Team members helping team leaders on shift

Fast and accurate service moving swift

Supervisor thinking bout promoting

Team members to team leaders, no floating

When you love what you do there's no failure

Love it when customers have large orders

At His Feet

As I bowed my head humble in despair

Needing His love for my heart to repair

Lowly in spirit when I call His name

The inner me enemy is the blame

And I've come to realize I am the tail

Trying to make Him proud, I know I've failed

Never have I wanted this to happen

Feel the wrath of God on me, He's snappin

Every punishment I do deserve

A place in hell for me, He has reserved

I lift my eyes to say, Jesus is King

A table of false hope is what I bring

Poem was written, I wasn't thinking straight

Ministering for Jesus with no faith

Drunken Worship

Like a cup overflow, He fills me up,

Intoxicated with praise and worship.

Hands lifted referencing God, Todah.

Moderation of His glory somehow.

Perform, telling Christ, whom He is to me,

The Lord, my banner, Jehovah-Nissi.

Plastered on the altar, humbled face down,

I drink living waters in Him, I drown.

One touch from Christ, I'm in adoration,

Needing a breakthrough, straight penetration.

Pay divine honor to life's Creator,

Everlasting God, faithful Creator.

I love on Him every chance I get,

Un-orthodox worship drunken spirit

Miscarrying the Word

On fire to witness yet a lost soul,

Carry the bible while there are lies told.

Testifying to help someone else through,

Miscarrying the word is what I do.

I've taught myself to speak amongst the crowd,

Speaking in unknown tongues and praying loud.

You saw me reading assumed I was deep,

Didn't realize I was half way asleep.

Practice what I preach because it's practice,

If they believe what's said, that's a tactic.

Misuse and take the Word out of context,

Birthing baby demons I don't regret.

Watered down so the itching ears can hear,

How I miscarry the Word with no fear.

Three Letters

These three letters represent what it is

How I can still enjoy my life and live

The first two letters, you took for a joke

I'm only human, that's me clearing smoke

In person or on paper which is best?

I'm tired of arguing and the stress

I wrote those letters to reveal my hurt

To tell you what it's like to dig up dirt

Would've wrote more so you can feel my pain

Ignore me if you want, it still won't change

It took time to write how you broke my heart

Why I wanted to be friends from the start

Carrying a Dead Man's Weight, reactive

It's like writing a pre-nub, contractive

Abort the Mission

I kept telling folks, I can't get pregnant,

Mad at self, cause to me it's important.

Walking round *Carrying a Dead Man's Weight*,

First unborn died, the truth I couldn't take.

What was I supposed to do, lose my mind?

It was spoken a year ago, due time.

January seventeenth I felt weak,

Wanted to say Hi but I couldn't speak.

Rolling from one side to the other side,

Thought about my unborn, laid down and cried.

I mean, I apologize it happened,

Call it saving face, know why it happened.

I cried cause I couldn't do nothing else,

I'm dead inside I did harm to myself.

Her Name Is Lorraine

Dragons, warlocks and spiritual killers

Weapons form against yet cannot kill her

Principalities seek to steal her soul

The fifth highest order of the nine fold

Prayer warrior she learned fasting is the key

Have faith while fasting in Christ, she is free

A woman who fears God honored by men

Woman of virtue, she sustains from sin

Family calls her blessed and sanctified

Satan gets mad when she wakes up to rise

Her hands are a gift; only God can give

Without the Holy Ghost she cannot live

Praise and worship release from her spirit

A praiser by nature, can you tell it?

Giant Giants

A city called Giant is far away

Fear in the people's heart for them to stay

Trust only in Christ if they were to move

Premeditated murder, it behooves

Woman and men on post even at night

They say, "fear not because the LORD will fight

This battle" as the enemy tumbles

Giant Giants, watch them all crumble

Every step another is deceased

Chains are falling and the people can breathe

Children are breaking family curses

Inner strength bulging out knowing your worth

In my mind some people still in that place

Hidden in plain sight without a trace.

Access Denied

Demonic spirits trying to kill me

Causing havoc where they go, guilty plea

Christ sees their dark ways, in a pot they're fried

Committing suicide, Access Denied

It's a real spiritual war going on

This goes further than who's right and who's wrong

I mean people out here recruiting souls

They tried to destroy me, the Lord said 'No'

Hear me when I say, BRAIN WASHING IS REAL

If you're a tither, your money they steal

Demon possessed, they need somewhere to live

Including the ones who Netflix and chill

It's simple things the devil starts to try

Opening gates, Christ said, "Access Denied"

‘Eleven

I’ve messed up a lot in this life of mine

But God put me back right every time

Two thousand eleven was my worst year

Walking with my chest out, there was no fear

Went to jail that year, cried like a baby

Whole year later, asked the Lord to save me

I swear, I don’t want to go back that far

Saw a man shot dead, that’s a mental scar

Wasn’t miserable but I was broke

Cigarettes or weed, I needed a smoke

Worked in fast food flipping burgers and chicks

Homie tried to lace me, his in-law sick

So turned out, even popped a few blue pills

Don’t get caught up trying to prove you real

Unexcused Absence

Friday through Tuesday were my excused days

Scheming on a plan and making some plays

It's been a year since I took a visit

Only five of us here, that's the remnant,

I cringe every time he says my name

Hit man loosed but hit man has now been tamed

The professionals don't know where I'm at

Workers told lies so they don't seem like rats

'Where's Jennifer? She's missing in action'

Somewhere throwing up unexcused absence.

"Call your job to make sure they know you're here."

Why? so they can joke and laugh at my fears?

But that's beside the point, I should've called

Not assuming writing can fix it all.

Sonnet for a Dead Man

It was November ninth two, thousand twelve

Best friend died like he gave up on himself

I said that cause we talked about so much

I can tell he was tired and gave up

Went to visit him in the hospital

He saw me cry when I saw him cripple

In them two years he showed me real friendship

Taught me how to roast; homie was a trip

Recorded videos on my YouTube

Remembering your voice, I miss you dude

Can't lie, them two weeks we ain't speak was dumb

Your girl was mad and my ex was a bum

Through everything our friendship stayed real

Six years you've been gone; it's been time to heal

On A Lighter Note

I've been smiling more now than I use to

Cause I don't go through the things I use to

Jesus has been manifesting my prayers

I'm feeling and looking better, all stares

Started back reading the Word, thank you Lord

Yall pray for me, let's get on one accord

On a Lighter Note: Christ has slowed me down

To appreciate His mercies around

I know my life won't ever be the same

I just don't want my prayers to be in vain

I'm close to my Associate's degree

My self-esteem ain't low that's major key

On a Lighter Note: my books are selling

Do yall hear the truth behind me yelling?

Spiritual Warfare

They knock on the door at night as I sleep

A dreamer of dreams at rest as they creep

Inside my bedroom, invisible cloak

They want to attack my heart with a stroke

Through the day I re-read Psalm 35

Thanking Jesus for keeping me alive

Nightly prayer restrains them, I’m protected

Survived the lion’s den or ejected

I plead the blood of Jesus to stay safe

The word of God is my spiritual mace

I don’t want to fight, they’ve made this a war

They remind me of my sins, sleeping whore

Following me just to catch me off guard

Incubus, succubus daytime discard

Connected To Wealth

Daughter of Christ, I'm connected to wealth

Blessings of prosperity and good health

Supernatural miracles taken place

First, seek the word of God everyday

Delight in His presence, Jesus our LORD

Living a life of sin, I can't afford

Connected to wealth, my Father is KING

Make a joyful noise in worship, I sing

Windows of heaven overtaken me

I'm blessed by the best continually

Heir to the throne, my connection is deep

When storms of life happen, I fall asleep

Jesus washed me clean, His blood saved my life

Through baptism, I'm connected to Christ

Coffee Shop Discussions

Don't let distractions take you away

From the hand of Christ, His mercy and grace

Stay focused through open doors and blessings

Remain faithful, be watchful for testings

Prayer is key to unlock obedience

Dot your eyes and cross your tees each sentence

Enjoy the journey and destinations

Take heed to the dreams and revelations

Jesus wants a confession day and night

His angels are ready for war to fight

Don't forget to fast before laying hands

For the word of God, I will take a stand

Be humble no matter how high you get

Jesus gives slowly, he takes away quick

Failed With Honor

Yeah, I'm saved but I don't want to fall short
Resist temptations, that's an extreme sport
Eat daily bread, I shouldn't disappoint
Walk past drug dealers offering their joint
Prove to be lack in what is expected
In their hometown, prophets are rejected
Fail: not fulfill the expectation of
I love people, the same way Jesus love
He must increase so I become weaker
I praise His name yet He looks for seekers
A sinner saved by grace, I fail daily
Christian schizophrenic, who's not crazy
How can I say I failed with honor?
When it comes to Jesus, I'm a runner

Alive Again

Only reason I've overcame giants
By the blood of Jesus keeping me saved
Preserved like Lazarus, brought from the grave
I was foolish in my sins, defiant
Blinded by the god of this world dying
Wanted to be free from flesh not a slave
None of my own work, Jesus gets the praise
Dead bones are no more, I am reliant
It takes repenting to be born again
Remorseful confession to Jesus Christ
Be baptized for the remission of sins
Remove the old man, new creature, new life
In book of Revelation, Jesus wins
I'm here to say, "Holiness is still right"

Waving My Flag

Do yall have coworkers you don't speak to?

But yall supposed to be thicker than glue

Why you stopped speaking, I have no idea

You was my inspiration, you stayed real

I called a few times but my number blocked

Can we start over or erase like chalk?

I understand why you holding a grudge

Sent a letter of reconcile, no budge.

Remember how you drove past me that day?

I thank Christ for it happening that way

I'm hoping you get to read this sonnet

No hard feelings over here, it's done with

Hopefully soon we'll be back on good terms

We family. This was a lesson learned.

Keep Up With My Social Media

Youtube.com/Mc08Nugget

Twitter - @WritingsFromJen

Instagram - @WritingsFromJen

Email: alexjen2008@gmail.com

Made in the USA
Middletown, DE
08 May 2021

39198093R10060